SCI-FAX

LEARN ABOUT
SCIENCE

Written by David Holzer

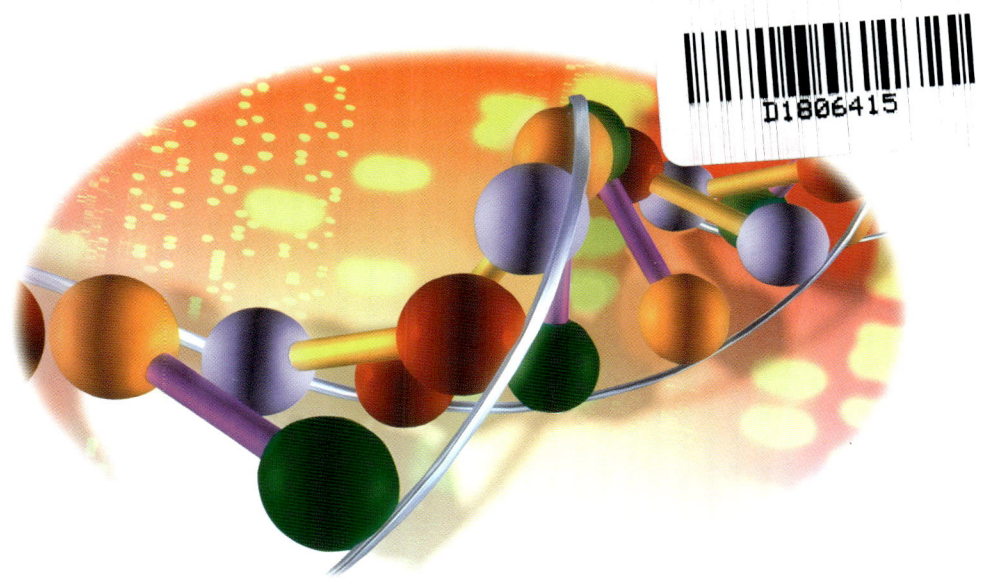

TOPTHAT!Kids™

Copyright © 2005 Top That! Publishing plc,
Tide Mill Way, Woodbridge, Suffolk IP12 1AP, UK
www.topthatpublishing.com
Top That! Kids is a trademark of Top That! Publishing plc

THERE ARE MANY DIFFERENT BRANCHES OF SCIENCE, AND THE RESULTS OF SCIENTIFIC RESEARCH AFFECT EVERY PART OF OUR LIVES. SCIENTISTS FOLLOW THE SAME PRINCIPLES TO CARRY OUT THEIR EXPERIMENTS AND CONDUCT RESEARCH. YOU CAN HAVE LOTS OF FUN LEARNING HOW TO THINK, AND ACT, LIKE A SCIENTIST.

EAGLE-EYED OBSERVATION

Good scientists are observant. They train themselves to look closely at everything around them. They're also curious. You should develop these qualities if you want to be a good scientist.

TAKING NOTES

When you take notes, try to:

- record everything important that you see;
- make notes as soon as you notice something;
- write your notes clearly; and
- keep your notes neat and tidy.

Good scientists observe their experiments very closely and note everything down, whatever the result.

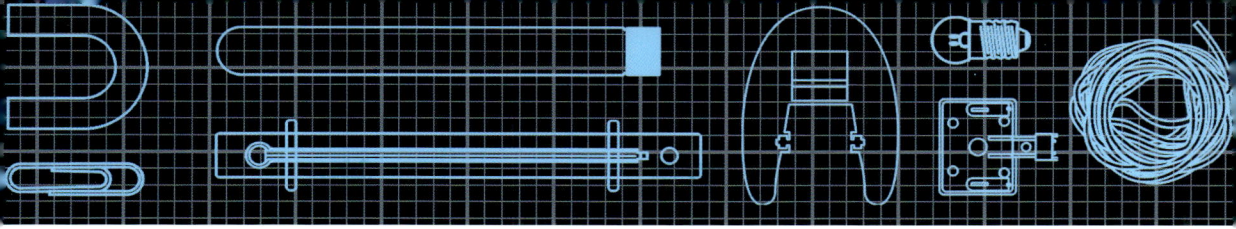

WHY EXPERIMENT?

When you carry out an experiment, it can be for many different reasons – to test an idea you may have, perhaps. Sometimes you could carry out the same experiment several times in order to prove a theory. Alternatively, you may carry out lots of experiments under one set of conditions and want to find out what happens if you change these conditions.

AMAZING DISCOVERIES

Many important scientific discoveries have been made completely by accident, from plastics and safety glass to nylon and Velcro™.

A man named George de Mestral invented Velcro™ after a chance discovery in the woods one day. He became annoyed by the burrs that stuck to his clothing as he was walking and wondered why they were so difficult to remove. When he looked closely, he saw that they had hook-like arms. Inspired, he invented a hook-and-loop fastener and called it Velcro™.

So, try to remain curious and observant, and maybe you'll make a great discovery!

Some types of trainers are fastened with Velcro™.

EXPERIMENTS THAT GO WRONG

If you don't set up an experiment correctly you might not get the results that you expect. You do everything the right way – you think – but something completely different happens.

This doesn't mean that your experiment has gone 'wrong'; it means that you could have discovered something unusual. How exciting!

CONDUCTING EXPERIMENTS CAN INVOLVE USING DELICATE EQUIPMENT, USING ELECTRICITY, HANDLING GLASS OR SHARP OBJECTS AND WORKING WITH CHEMICALS THAT COULD POSSIBLY HURT YOU IF YOU'RE NOT VERY CAREFUL. IT'S IMPORTANT TO CARRY OUT ALL EXPERIMENTS IN 100% SAFE CONDITIONS.

BEING SENSIBLE

Whatever kind of experiment you're conducting, please make sure you will be safe at all times. If you are not sure whether an experiment is dangerous or safe, always ask an adult.

USING EQUIPMENT

Equipment is often very delicate and easy to damage, so always use it carefully. If you damage any equipment, you can't be sure that the results of your experiments are correct.

Always tell an adult before you start experimenting.

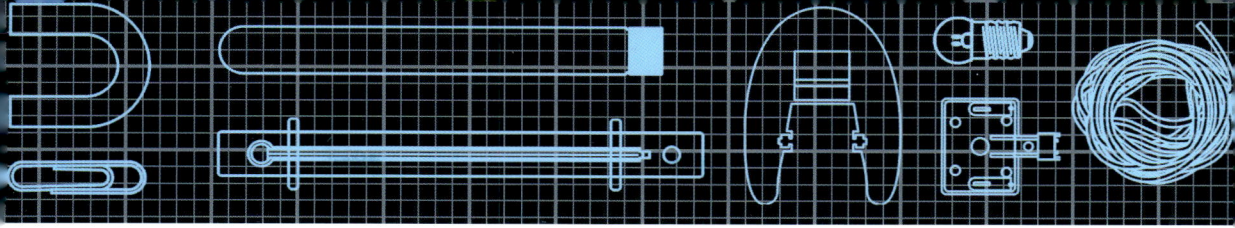

WORKING WITH CHEMICALS

None of the experiments in this book use dangerous chemicals but, if you want to carry out other experiments, please be very careful using chemicals. Never put chemicals in your mouth, always wash your hands, and make sure you store any chemicals safely in clearly labelled containers.

SHARP OBJECTS

Scientists often use sharp objects, such as scalpels, in their experiments. Whenever you're cutting something up – to mount it on a slide, perhaps – please be very careful.

USING ELECTRICITY

Whenever an experiment involves electricity, or using electrical equipment, make sure that the experiment is conducted away from water and that you're not going to trip over any cables or leads.

USING BATTERIES

Fit the batteries correctly using the + and – direction as indicated on the battery.

Non-rechargeable batteries should not be recharged.

Only batteries of the same type as recommended are to be used.

Exhausted batteries must be removed.

Do not mix old and new batteries.

Do not mix alkaline, standard, or rechargeable batteries.

Do not place batteries in water or near extreme heat.

The supply terminals must not be short-circuited.

Scientists always take care when using chemicals.

BIOLOGY IS THE STUDY OF ALL LIVING THINGS ON EARTH, FROM THE TINIEST ORGANISMS THAT CAN ONLY BE SEEN WITH A MICROSCOPE TO THE WORLD'S LARGEST ANIMALS. LIFE EXISTS IN MANY DIFFERENT FORMS AND SCIENTISTS STUDY THEM TO FIND OUT HOW THEY WORK AND INTERACT WITH ONE ANOTHER.

CELLS

All living things are made up of cells and every cell contains a nucleus and cytoplasm enclosed by membrane. Cells are like tiny factories where chemical reactions take place. These reactions, such as converting food into energy, help keep the organism alive. Some organisms, such as amoebas, are made up of just one cell, whereas more advanced organisms consist of a variety of specialised cells which make up tissues and organs that perform specific functions.

DNA

Buried inside the nucleus of each cell there is a chemical 'code' which gives the organism its unique characteristics. This code is held in a spiral-shaped molecule that we know as DNA – deoxyribonucleic acid. Each strand of DNA contains many separate instructions, or genes, and each gene controls a different characteristic – eye colour, for example.

The double helix (spiral) shape of the DNA molecule was discovered in 1953 by James Watson and Francis Crick.

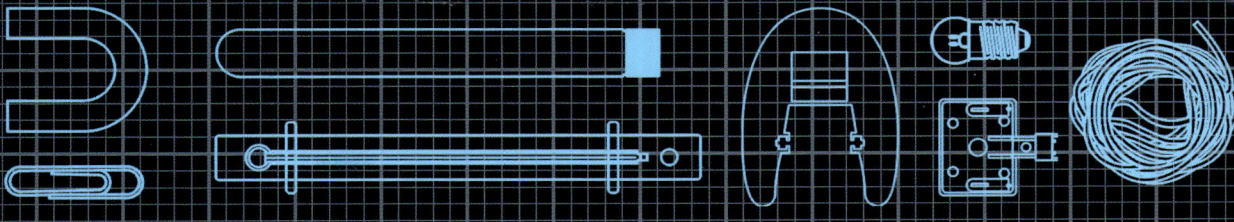

PHOTOSYNTHESIS EXPERIMENT

YOU WILL NEED

- a plant with large leaves
- paper
- sticky tape
- scissors

I. Cut the paper into small pieces. Stick a few pieces onto the plant's leaves. Leave the plant for a few days, ensuring that it is watered and receives plenty of light.

2. After a few days, remove the pieces of paper. The leaves will have withered where the paper was stuck.

HOW DOES IT WORK?

Most plants are made from special cells containing chlorophyll – a green chemical that can trap light energy from the Sun and convert it into food for the plant. This process is called photosynthesis. By taping pieces of paper onto the plant's leaves, the light was blocked and, no longer able to photosynthesize, the covered areas began to die.

THIS VERY SIMPLE EXPERIMENT SHOWS HOW PLANTS ABSORB WATER FROM EARTH AND RELEASE IT INTO THE ATMOSPHERE SO THAT IT CAN BE USED AGAIN.

WATER IN EARTH'S ATMOSPHERE

Did you know that it's impossible to create water? The water on Earth, in the atmosphere and inside plants and animals is constantly recycled. When plants absorb water through their roots and release it, it's called transpiration.

A GARDEN THAT WATERS ITSELF

YOU WILL NEED
• a large jar with a lid
• a ruler
• gravel
• crumbly soil
• two long sticks
• a small plant and moss
• a jug of water

I. Measure 2 cm of gravel into the jar and pour 2 cm of soil on top. Make a hole in the middle of the soil using one of the sticks.

2 cm
2 cm

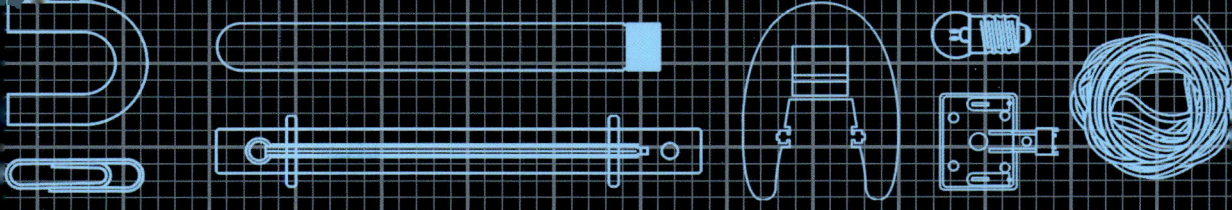

2. Pick up the plant between your two sticks (as if you're using chopsticks) and lower it into the hole. Use your sticks to push the soil down around it. Finally, add the moss, then pour in water until the soil is wet.

3. Leave the jar open for three days. Some of the water will evaporate, helping the plant draw up water through its roots. Seal the jar and watch the plant grow.

Water lost by transpiration

Water absorbed by the roots

Water falls to the ground

The transpiration process.

HOW DOES IT WORK?

You'll notice that water transpiring through the leaves gathers on the jar and then runs back down into the soil. The garden is recycling the water and watering itself! Remove the seal once a week for an hour and the plant will grow to fill the jar.

ALL SOUND IS PRODUCED BY THINGS VIBRATING. WHEN SOMETHING VIBRATES, IT MAKES THE AIR AROUND IT EXPAND AND CONTRACT. THIS MOVEMENT CREATES SOUND WAVES WHICH TRAVEL THROUGH THE AIR. SOUND WAVES ARE ALSO ABLE TO TRAVEL THROUGH SOLID OBJECTS.

SOUND WAVES

Sound is a type of energy that can only be made by something moving. Whether that 'something' is a solid, a liquid or a gas, its molecules are pushed and pulled, passing energy along in the shape of a wave. As the molecules collide, tiny amounts of energy are lost. This means that both the wave and the sound gradually fade with distance.

HOW WE HEAR

Our outer ears are designed to direct sound waves into the eardrum. The eardrum vibrates and the vibrations are passed through a number of tiny bones to a tube called the cochlea. Fluid inside the cochlea vibrates and stimulates special hairs connected to nerves. The nerves send signals to the brain which are translated into sounds that we recognise.

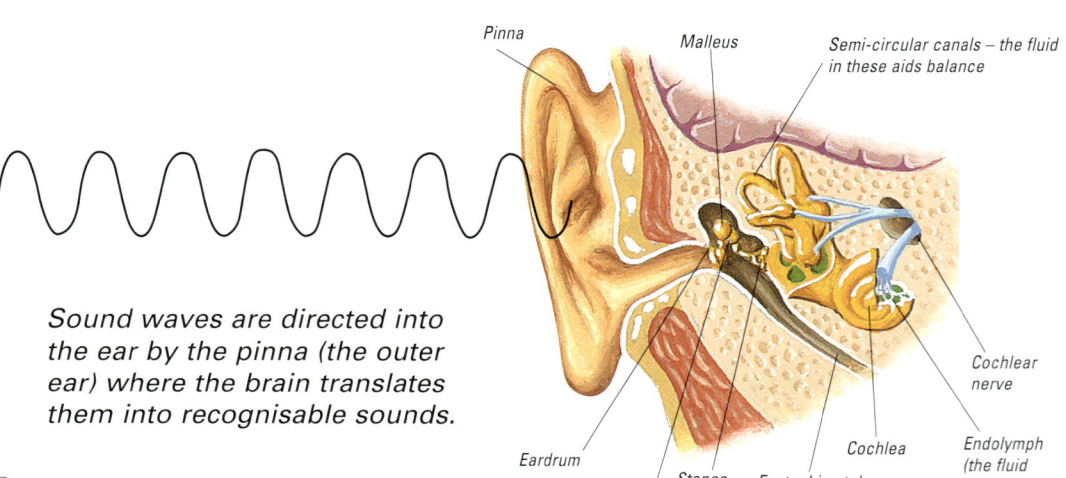

Pinna

Malleus

Semi-circular canals – the fluid in these aids balance

Sound waves are directed into the ear by the pinna (the outer ear) where the brain translates them into recognisable sounds.

Cochlear nerve

Eardrum

Incus

Stapes

Eustachian tube

Cochlea

Endolymph (the fluid that vibrates)

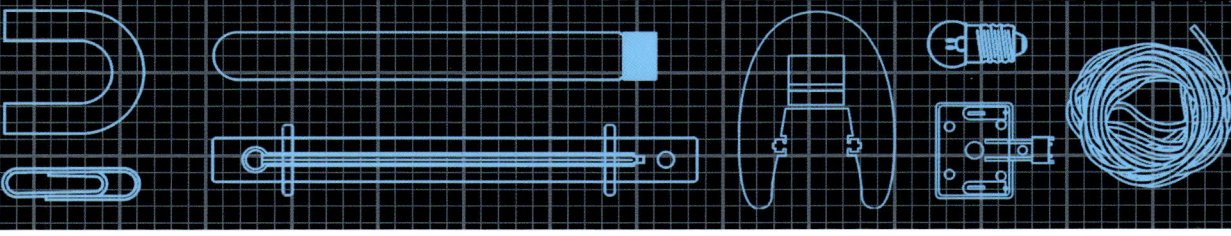

MAKE A CUP PHONE

YOU WILL NEED

- two plastic cups or clean yoghurt pots
- a piece of string (2 m long)
- scissors

1. Ask an adult to help you make a small hole in the bottom of each cup.

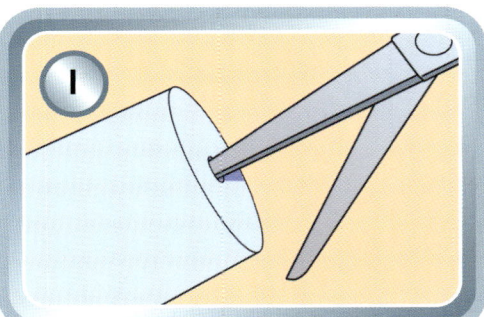

2. Poke one end of the string through the hole of one cup and tie a knot. Repeat with the other cup.

3. Hold one cup yourself and ask a friend to take the other.

4. Pull the string tight between you and ask your friend to speak into their cup while you put your ear to yours.

HOW DOES IT WORK?

The sound waves made by your friend's voice made the string vibrate. When the vibrations reached your ear, your eardrum also vibrated and told your brain that you had heard a noise.

ACIDS AND ALKALIS ARE NATURALLY OCCURRING SUBSTANCES THAT REACT WITH OTHERS, SUCH AS WATER. WHEN ACIDS AND ALKALIS ARE MIXED TOGETHER, THEY CANCEL EACH OTHER OUT. THE STRENGTH OF AN ACID OR ALKALI CAN BE MEASURED USING THE PH SCALE.

SOME ACIDS AND ALKALIS

Your stomach contains hydrochloric acid, a very powerful corrosive acid that helps to break down food. Indigestion tablets are alkaline, which is why they cancel out the excess acid in your stomach.

Bee stings contain strong acids, and wasp stings alkalis, which is why it hurts if you are stung. Soap is a common type of alkali, and soaps and detergents work by breaking down the acids in oils.

The pH scale measures the acidity or alkaline level of a solution. It's very easy to make your own pH indicator.

Soap – a common alkaline substance.

DID YOU KNOW?

Industrial gases in the atmosphere react with water in the air to produce acid which can then fall as acid rain. Acid rain can corrode some stone buildings, metals and also damage trees.

Acid rain corrodes metal.

Wasp stings contain strong alkalis.

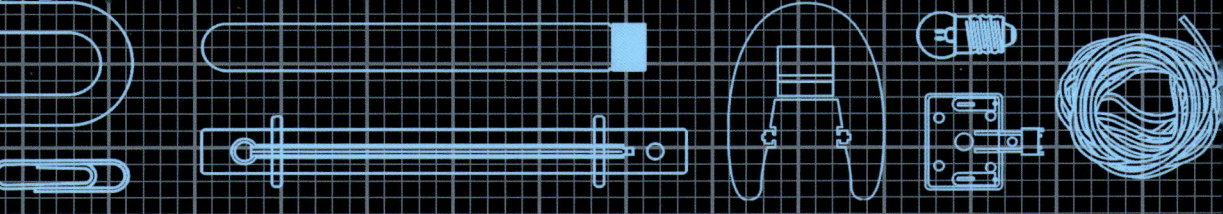

MAKE YOUR OWN PH INDICATOR

YOU WILL NEED

- half a red cabbage
- a grater or blender
- a saucepan
- a colander
- a jar
- a test tube or egg cup
- acid and alkali solutions to test – try vinegar, lemon juice or washing-up liquid

1. Grate the cabbage into small pieces or put it in a blender.

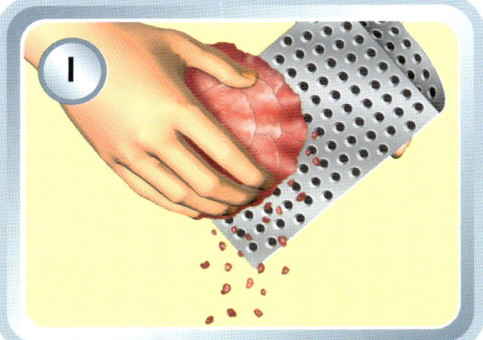

WARNING

Ask an adult to help you heat the water.

2. Put the grated cabbage into a saucepan, cover it with water, then boil it for 20–30 minutes until it turns dark purple. Strain the liquid into the jar.

3. Pour some of your test solution into the test tube or egg cup. Add some cabbage juice and watch what happens to the colour.

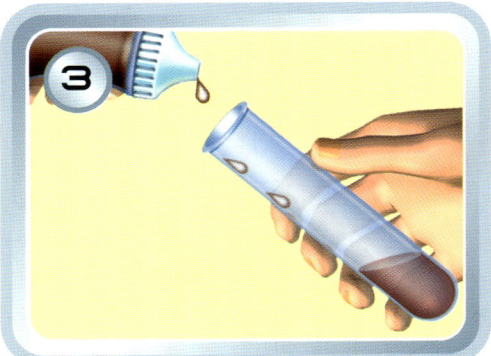

4. Make a record of your findings, then rinse the test tube before trying another test solution.

13

UNDERSTANDING THE PH SCALE

In order to measure the acidity or alkalinity of a substance, scientists test solutions with litmus paper and compare the results to the pH scale.

When reading the pH scale, the most acidic substances will have a pH value of 0, the most alkaline will have a pH value of 14, while neutral substances, such as pure water, will have a pH value of 7.

Litmus comes from lichen plants – in its natural state it is blue.

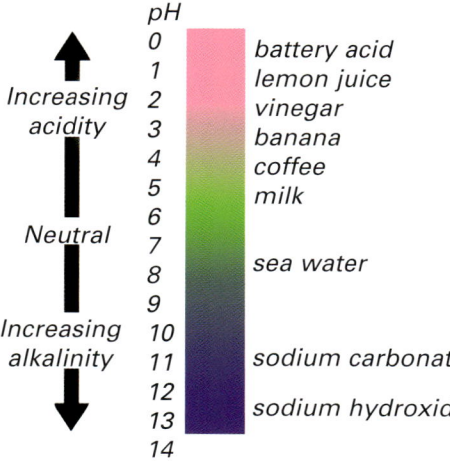

pH

0 — battery acid
1 — lemon juice
2 — vinegar
3 — banana
4 — coffee
5 — milk
6
7
8 — sea water
9
10
11 — sodium carbonate
12
13 — sodium hydroxide
14

Increasing acidity

Neutral

Increasing alkalinity

The pH scale.

MAKE YOUR OWN LITMUS PAPER

To make your own litmus paper, all you need to do is soak a piece of blotting paper, or coffee filter paper, in cabbage juice and leave it to dry.

To find out the pH value of a substance, soak the litmus paper in the test solution, then leave the paper to dry. When the paper is dry it will have changed to a colour that corresponds to a numerical value on the pH scale.

Acidic substances produce a pink colour and alkaline substances produce a purple colour. Neutral substances will turn the litmus paper green.

Lemon juice will turn the litmus paper pink.

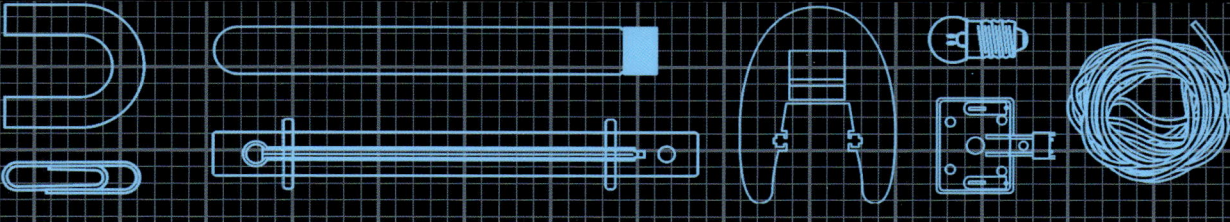

MIXING FOR EXPLOSIVE RESULTS

YOU WILL NEED

- vinegar
- baking soda (not baking powder)
- a bottle
- a cork to fit in the bottle

I. Put some of the baking soda in the bottle and add some vinegar.

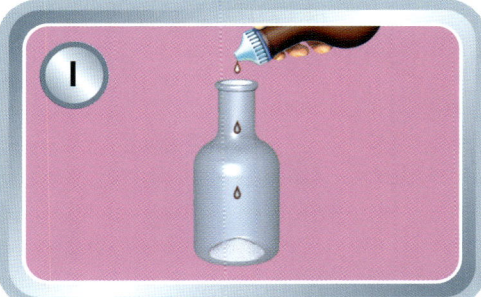

2. As soon as the mixture starts fizzing, put the cork in.

WARNING

Be sure to hold the bottle so that the cork is nowhere near your face, anyone else, or anything breakable.

3. Stand back and watch what happens!

HOW DOES IT WORK?

The vinegar (an acid) neutralises the baking soda (an alkali). This creates a reaction that produces a gas (carbon dioxide). This gas causes the fizzing, and the build-up of gas makes the cork pop out.

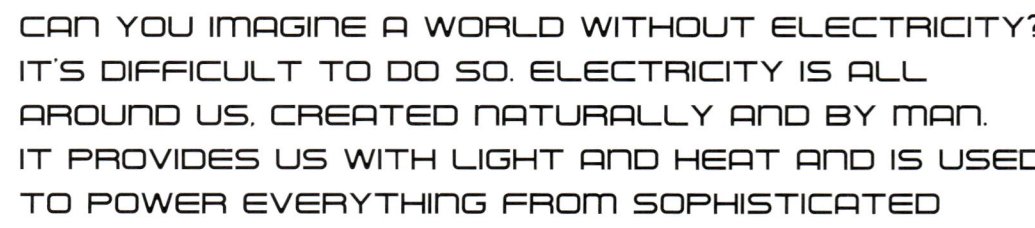

CAN YOU IMAGINE A WORLD WITHOUT ELECTRICITY? IT'S DIFFICULT TO DO SO. ELECTRICITY IS ALL AROUND US, CREATED NATURALLY AND BY MAN. IT PROVIDES US WITH LIGHT AND HEAT AND IS USED TO POWER EVERYTHING FROM SOPHISTICATED COMPUTERS TO ELECTRIC TOASTERS.

ELECTRIC CURRENT

Atoms contain protons with a positive charge and electrons with a negative charge. Batteries and generators separate the protons and electrons so that the electrons start to flow from one atom to another, creating an electric current.

A multimeter can be used to measure electric current.

RESISTANCE

The measure of how easily electric current flows through a material is called resistance. Light bulbs work using filaments – the wires inside the bulb – that have a high level of resistance. Electricity finds it hard to flow through them, so they heat up and produce light.

Electricity encounters resistance in the filaments of a light bulb, causing them to heat up and produce light.

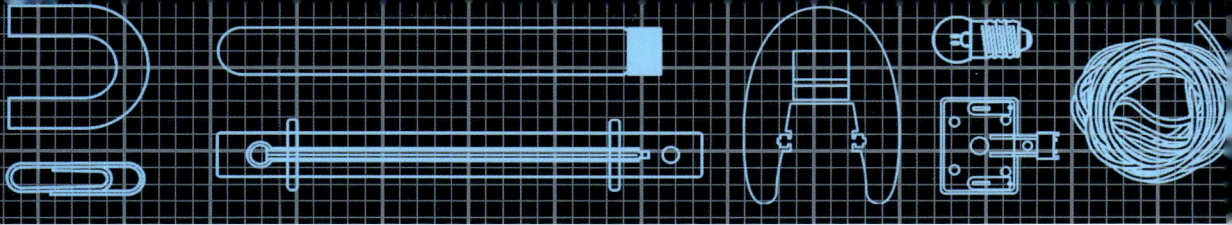

MAKE THE STEADY HAND GAME

YOU WILL NEED

- a pair of pliers
- an uncoated wire hanger
- 25 cm insulated copper wire
- sticky tape
- scissors
- a bulb and bulb holder
- a small screw driver
- two electrical lead wires with alligator clips at each end
- a battery casing and two AA batteries
- a block of wood measuring about 50 cm x 20 cm
- wire staples
- a hammer

WARNING

Ask an adult to help you make the steady hand game. Beware of sharp points – the wire hanger, the insulated wire and the staples may be sharp.

I. Use the pliers to cut a 6 cm length from the wire hanger. Bend it into an open loop, as shown. This is the piece you will hold to test how steady your hand is!

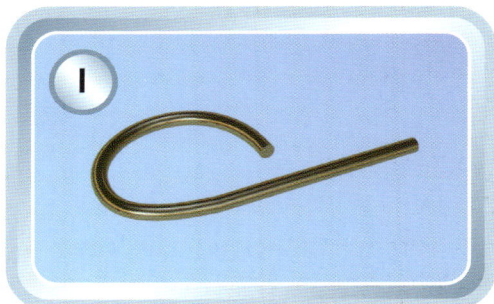

2. Ask an adult to help you strip 2.5 cm from each end of the insulated copper wire. Wind one end of the wire around the loop made in step 1, securing it with sticky tape if necessary. Attach the other end to the bulb holder – tighten the screw to keep it in place.

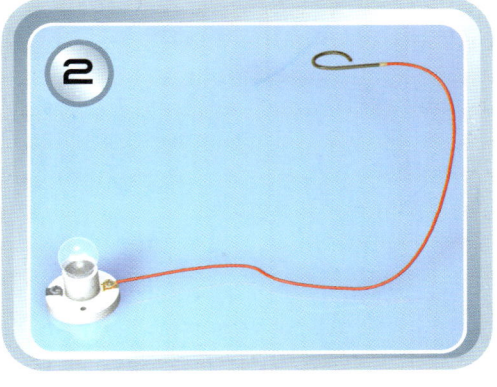

3. Clip a piece of electrical lead wire to one of the battery casing wires and to the free screw on the bulb holder.

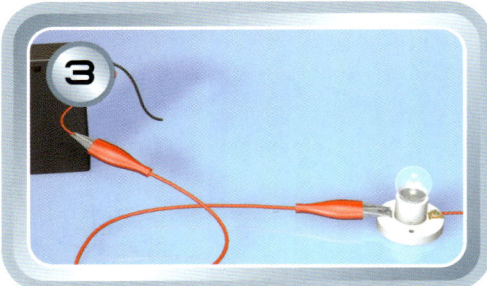

4. Wrap sticky tape around the ends of the remaining hanger wire. Bend the wire into a wavy shape – make it as complicated as you like.

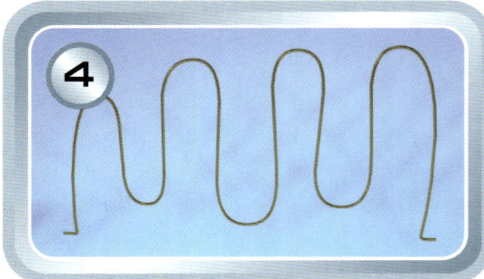

5. Hammer the staples over the ends of the wavy wire, securing it to the block of wood.

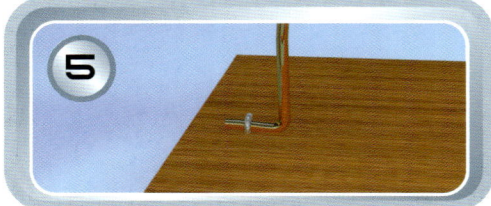

6. Clip one end of the remaining electrical lead wire to the wire hanger and the other end to the free battery casing wire.

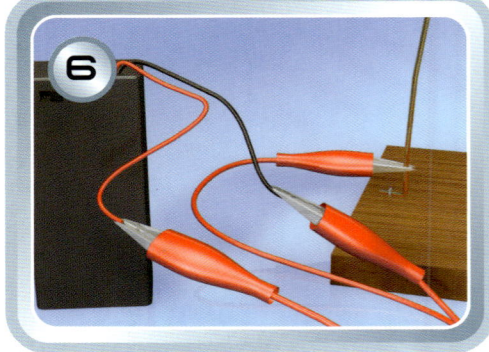

7. Bend the open loop around one end of the wavy wire, then close up the loop with the pliers.

8. Insert the batteries into the battery casing and make sure it is turned on. Now you're ready to play! As you've probably guessed, the aim is to move the loop all the way along the wavy wire without the two touching.

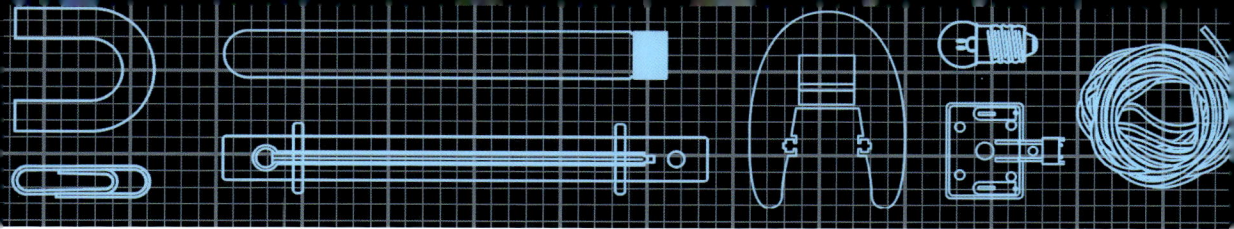

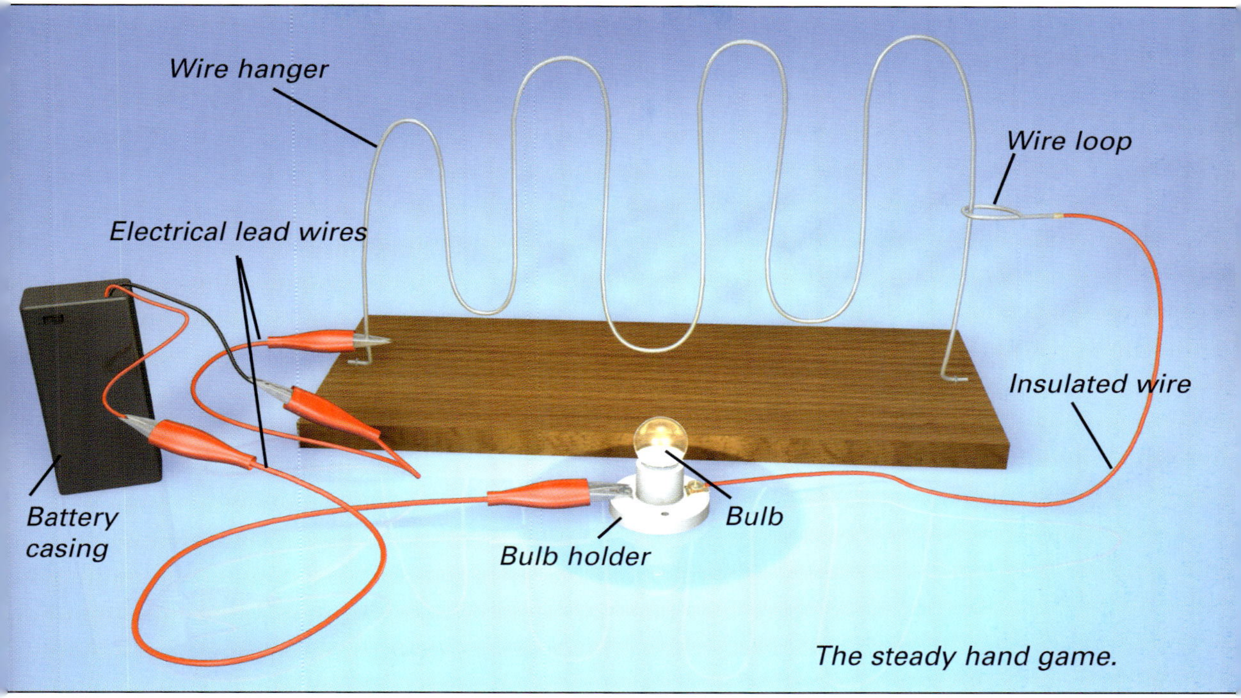

Wire hanger

Wire loop

Electrical lead wires

Insulated wire

Battery
casing

Bulb

Bulb holder

The steady hand game.

HOW DOES IT WORK?

An electrical current needs a continuous path in order to flow. This path is called a circuit. In the steady hand game, a circuit is made when the wire loop touches the wire hanger – the current flows around the circuit and this is what makes the bulb light up. An electrical current won't flow if the path is broken. If you're good at the game, you won't touch the wire, which means the circuit is never completed so the bulb doesn't light up.

WHEN YOU'RE CONDUCTING A SENSITIVE EXPERIMENT, YOU MIGHT NOT WANT TO BE DISTURBED. YOU CAN USE ELECTRICITY TO MAKE A DOOR ENTRY SYSTEM TO LET PEOPLE KNOW WHETHER THEY CAN COME IN OR NOT.

MAKE A DOOR ENTRY SYSTEM

YOU WILL NEED

- a cardboard tube
- tinfoil
- two pieces of cardboard measuring 5 cm x 10 cm
- a piece of cardboard measuring 12 cm x 20 cm
- a red and a green LED
- red and green cellophane
- insulated copper wire
- a battery casing and two AA batteries
- two electrical lead wires with alligator clips at each end
- three drawing pins
- one paperclip
- three small corks
- scissors
- glue
- sticky tape

I. Cut the cardboard tube into two pieces, each about 7 cm long. Cut a small, square hole about half-way down each of these tubes.

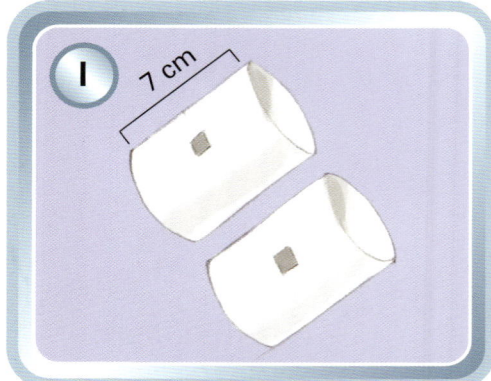

2. Glue tinfoil, shiny side up, to one side of a 5 cm x 10 cm piece of cardboard. Cut out two disks to fit tightly inside the tubes.

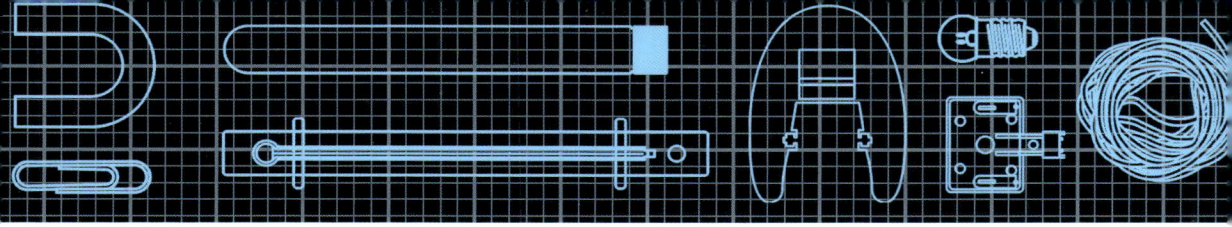

3. Cut slits in the centre of the two disks, and push an LED into each with the bulb on the foil side. Turn the disks over and spread the prongs on each of the LEDs to hold them firmly in place.

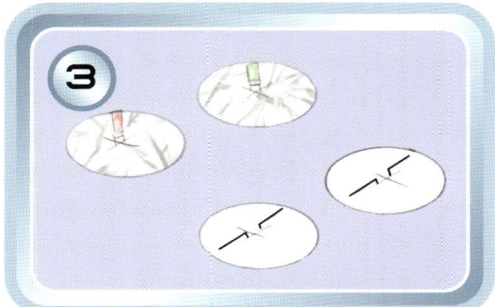

5. Push a disk into each tube and wedge it inside, about halfway down. Feed the wire out of the hole in the side of the tube.

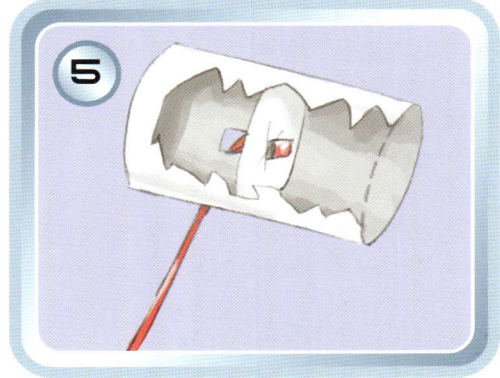

4. Cut two pieces of insulated wire 15 cm long and bare the ends. Tape one of the bare ends of each wire to one of the prongs on each of the LEDs.

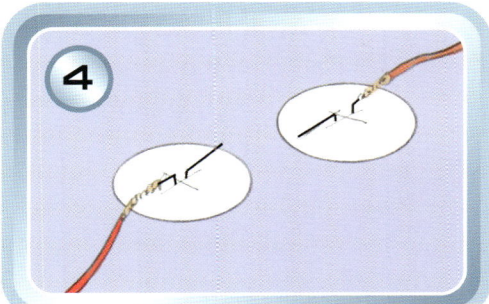

6. Cut three pieces of insulated wire long enough to reach loosely from the door to where the switch will be. Bare the ends, and put one wire aside. Tape a long wire to each of the remaining prongs on the back of the LED disks.

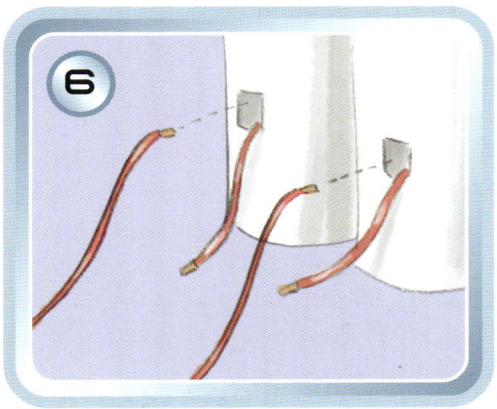

WARNING
Ask an adult to help you.

7. To make the panel that will hold your lights onto the doorframe, cut two circular holes in the 12 cm x 20 cm piece of cardboard, one above the other, big enough for the tubes to fit snugly.

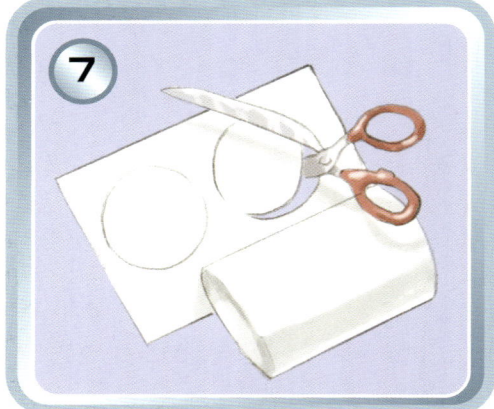

8. Push the back of the tube holding the red LED a little way into the top hole and the back of the tube holding the green LED into the bottom hole.

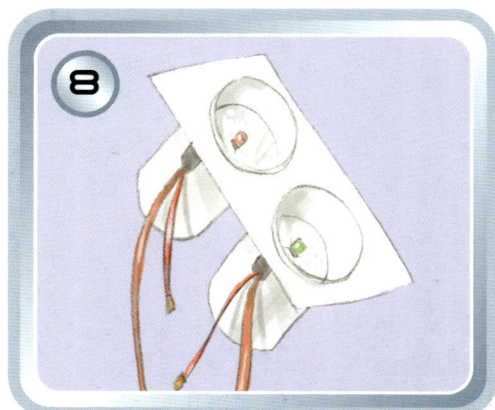

9. Twist together one end of the third long wire (known as the common wire) with the free ends of the two short wires. Tape the common wire and the other two long wires to the panel, to support their weight.

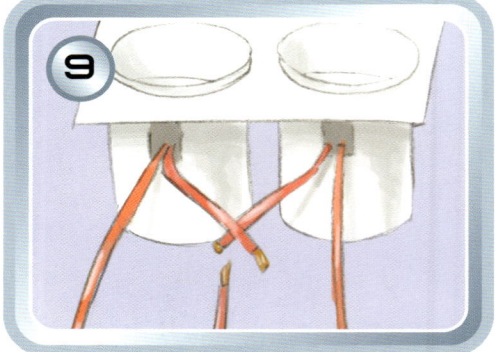

10. Tape the red piece of cellophane over the end of the tube at the top of the panel and the green piece over the tube at the bottom. Attach the panel firmly outside your room near the hinged side of the door.

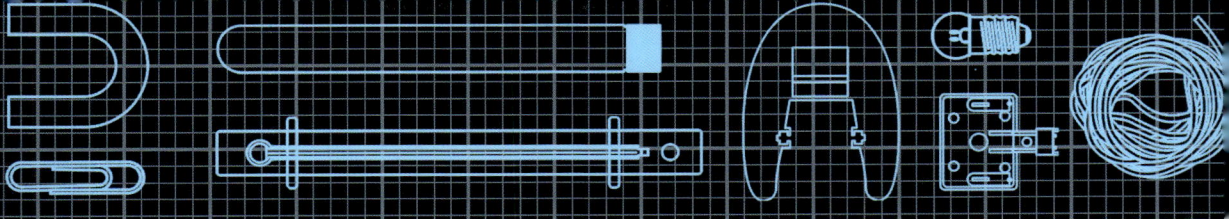

INSIDE YOUR ROOM

I. Feed the three long wires inside your room. Close the door, making sure it doesn't trap the wires. Attach one end of an electrical lead wire to the common wire, and the other end to one of the battery casing wires.

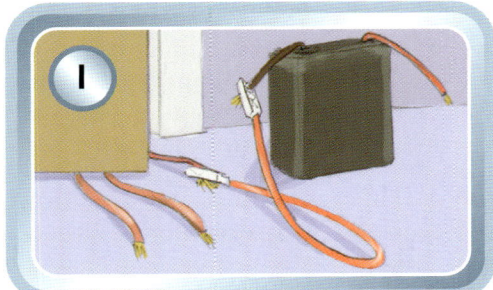

2. Stick three drawing pins into the remaining 5 cm x 10 cm piece of cardboard, pushing their points into the corks. Open out the paperclip and attach it to the middle pin. Check that the clip can touch the other two drawing pins, one at a time.

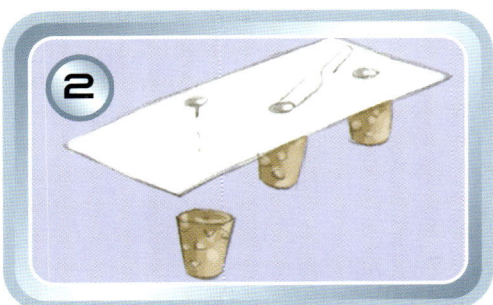

3. Clip one end of the remaining electrical lead wire to the pin holding the paperclip and the other end to the free battery casing wire. Wind the free ends of the two long wires around each of the other drawing pins.

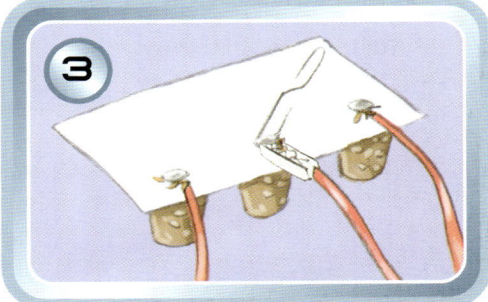

4. Try the switch. See which bulb lights in which position. Label the drawing pin for the red light 'Do Not Enter' and for the green light, 'Enter'.

Note: LEDs only work one way. If yours do not light first time, try changing the wires over.

HEAT AND TEMPERATURE

A THERMOMETER IS AN INSTRUMENT THAT MEASURES THE TEMPERATURE OF THINGS – HOW HOT OR COLD THEY ARE. TEMPERATURES ARE MEASURED IN FAHRENHEIT AND CELSIUS, AND SCIENTISTS OFTEN USE A MEASURE CALLED KELVIN.

THE HEAT METER

The name thermometer comes from 'thermo' meaning heat, and 'meter' meaning to measure.

Galileo, better known for discovering that Earth and the planets rotate around the Sun, is believed to have used a device called a thermometer in about 1600.

Galileo was one of the first scientists to use a thermometer.

TEMPERATURE TEST EXPERIMENT

YOU WILL NEED
- four clean, empty jars
- a tray
- a large jug
- one cotton glove or sock
- one woollen glove or sock
- a large piece of paper
- tinfoil
- a thermometer

I. Put the jars onto the tray and ask an adult to fill them with hot water.

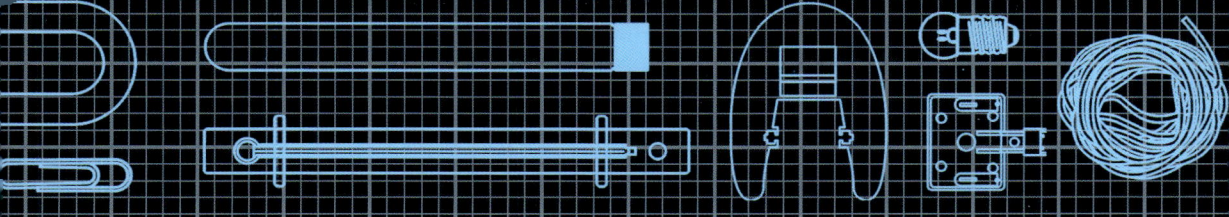

2. Carefully put the gloves or socks over two of the jars. Then carefully wrap the other two, one in paper and the other in tinfoil.

3. Leave the tray outside in the cold for about twenty minutes, then take the temperatures of each jar with the thermometer.

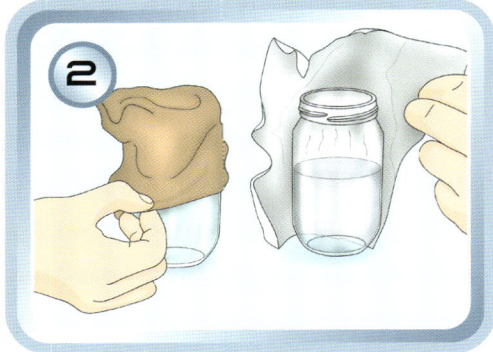

INSULATION

Which jar stayed the hottest? Which is now the coldest?

You should find that the jars covered in the tinfoil and the woollen glove or sock were the warmest. The jars covered in paper and the cotton glove or sock should have lost their heat more quickly. This shows that tinfoil and wool keep the heat in and can be called good insulators. Why not try this experiment with other materials you think might be good insulators?

CRYSTALS

CRYSTALS ARE CLEAR, COLOURLESS MINERALS WITH STRAIGHT EDGES AND FLAT FACES. IF A CRYSTAL LOOKS COLOURED, IT'S BECAUSE IT ABSORBS LIGHT IN A CERTAIN KIND OF WAY. THERE ARE MANY DIFFERENT TYPES OF CRYSTALS, FROM EVERYDAY SUBSTANCES SUCH AS SUGAR AND SALT, TO DIAMONDS AND QUARTZ.

WARNING

When handling chemicals, make sure there's an adult around. Always wash your hands afterwards.

Some crystals, such as diamonds, are quite rare and are used in expensive jewellery.

MAKE A SEED CRYSTAL

YOU WILL NEED

- 200 g of alum powder (which can be bought from a chemist's shop)
- a saucepan and a spoon
- a mug
- a saucer
- a large jar
- a cloth
- a pencil
- long thread

Crystals come in many different shapes and sizes. Some are so small that they can only be seen through a microscope. Others grow to be bigger than a human! Follow these instructions to make your own crystal. How big will it grow?

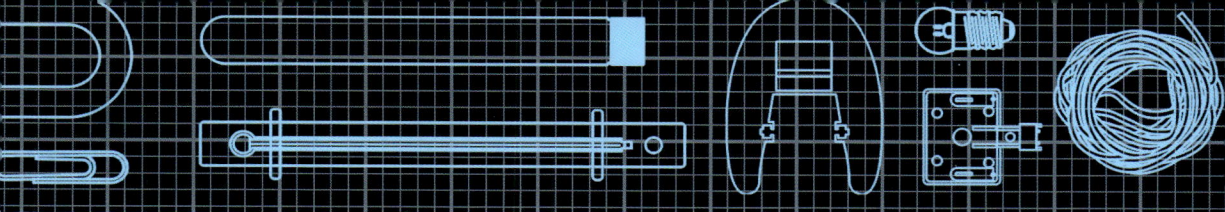

1. Put half the alum powder into the saucepan. Pour 2 mugs of water into the saucepan with the alum powder. Stir the solution until it is mixed well.

2. Ask an adult to help you heat the solution. Warm it gently, stirring it regularly. Add the extra alum powder until no more will dissolve. When it's ready, let the solution cool.

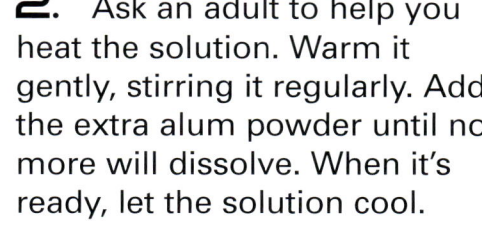

There are six basic shapes of crystal: 1) triclinic, 2) orthorhombic, 3) monoclinic, 4) hexagonal, 5) cubic and 6) tetragonal.

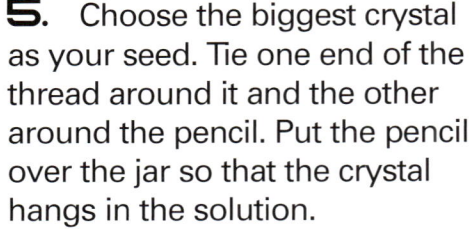

3. Pour some of the solution onto the saucer. Stand the saucer in a cool, dry place. Small crystals should form after a few days. Leave the saucer until all the solution has evaporated.

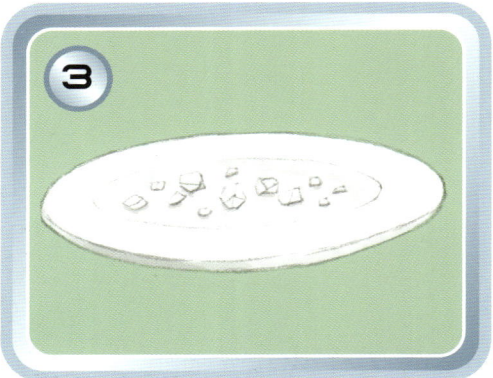

5. Choose the biggest crystal as your seed. Tie one end of the thread around it and the other around the pencil. Put the pencil over the jar so that the crystal hangs in the solution.

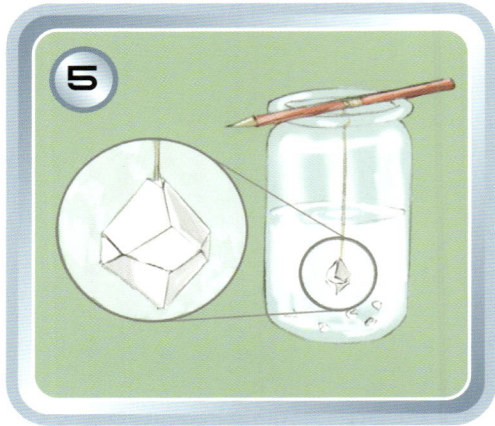

4. Pour the rest of the solution into the jar. Stir one more teaspoon of alum powder into the jar. Cover the jar with a cloth and leave it to one side until the crystals are ready.

HOW DOES IT WORK?

Crystals grow by a process called 'nucleation'. This begins when a solution is saturated (no more of the chemical can be dissolved) and solid material begins to form. This is how your experiment will work – it will take about three weeks to complete.

MAKE YOUR OWN STALACTITES AND STALAGMITES

Stalactites sometimes grow from the roofs of caves. Stalagmites grow upwards from the floor. They're both made from minerals that drip through the cave.

YOU WILL NEED

- two jars
- baking powder
- cotton thread or string
- washers or nails
- a saucer

Thousands of years of dripping water caused these impressive stalactites.

I. Fill the jars with hot water and add as much baking powder as will dissolve. Dip an end of the thread into each jar. Weight the ends of the thread with washers or nails and let the thread hang over the saucer.

2. Capillary action will draw the solution up through the thread and it will drip onto the saucer. In a few days, the dripping water will deposit the baking powder, forming tiny stalactites and stalagmites.

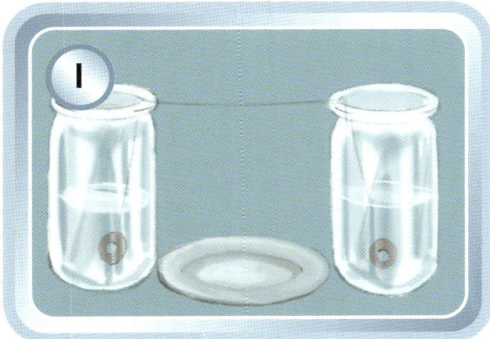

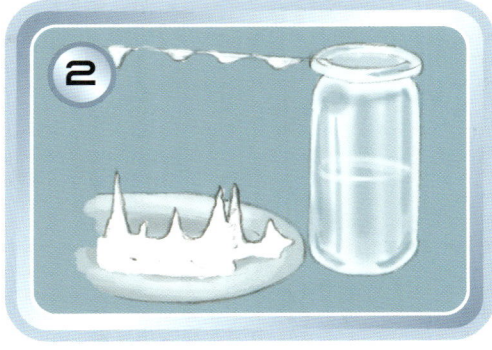

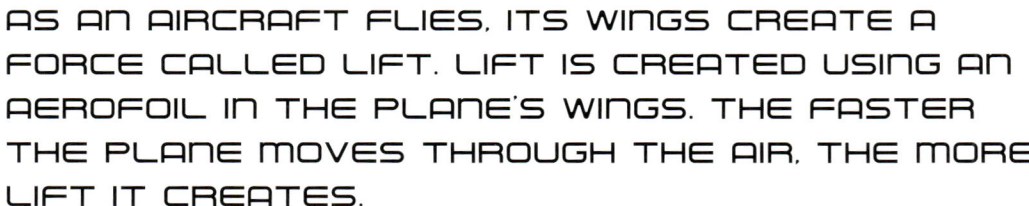

AS AN AIRCRAFT FLIES, ITS WINGS CREATE A FORCE CALLED LIFT. LIFT IS CREATED USING AN AEROFOIL IN THE PLANE'S WINGS. THE FASTER THE PLANE MOVES THROUGH THE AIR, THE MORE LIFT IT CREATES.

MAKE YOUR OWN FLYING WING

I. Fold the paper widthways leaving about 1.5 cm overlapping at the end. Cut holes in the paper 8 cm apart, 5 cm from the folded edge.

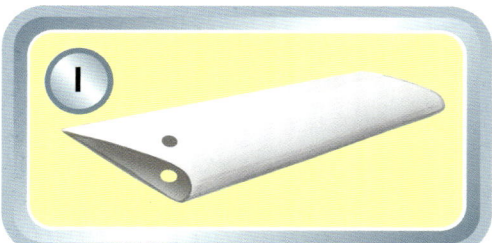

YOU WILL NEED

- a piece of stiff paper measuring 30 cm x 15 cm
- a cutting surface, such as a breadboard
- a sharp knife
- scissors
- a drinking straw
- two knitting needles
- a hair dryer
- sticky putty
- sticky tape

2. Tape the ends of the paper together to make a wing shape. Cut two 2.5 cm lengths of straw and push them through the holes.

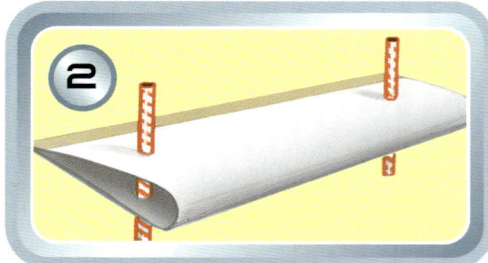

The shape of the wings is crucial in keeping this B-2 bomber airborne.

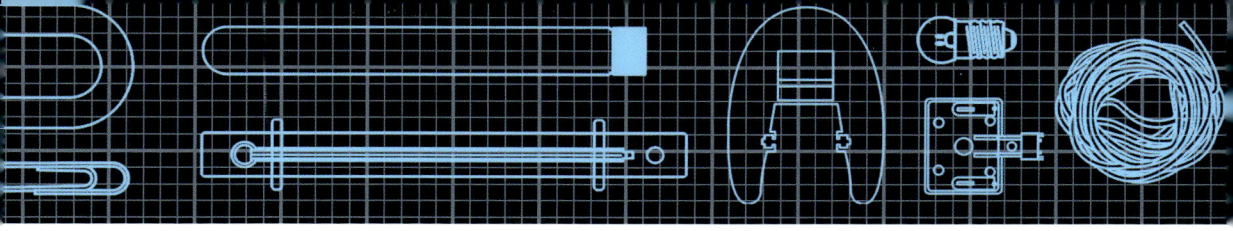

3. Stick the knitting needles through the straws and push them into the sticky putty. Make sure the wing has its curved surface on top.

4. Blow air at the front of the wing using the hair dryer, experimenting until you get it right and the wing rises.

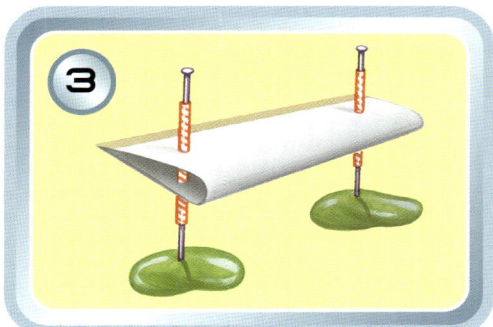

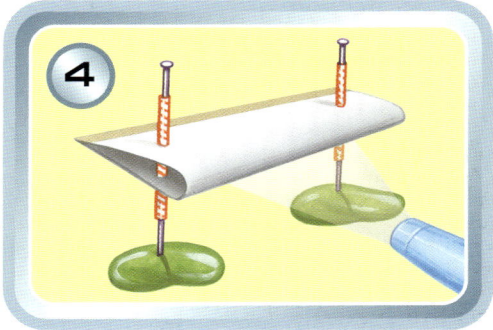

AERODYNAMICS

An aeroplane's wings are shaped to allow air to flow faster on the curved upper surface, so creating a higher pressure underneath. This generates a force directed upwards, which holds the aeroplane in the air. The lift created by the air flowing over the wings counterbalances the weight of the plane and the natural downwards force of gravity.

This Eurofighter's wings use the same principle as your own flying wing.

MAGNETISM

MAGNETISM IS A VERY POWERFUL FORCE THAT PULLS ON SOME METALS, SUCH AS IRON AND STEEL. IT WILL ALSO TRAVEL THROUGH THINGS THAT AREN'T MAGNETIC, SUCH AS CARDBOARD, GLASS, PLASTIC AND EVEN WATER.

MAKE NEEDLE MAGNETS

YOU WILL NEED

- two needles
- a horseshoe magnet
- drawing pins

You can use horseshoe magnets to make other magnetic materials become magnets themselves. Make these needle magnets, then use them for other experiments.

Which of these items will your magnet pick up?

I. Hold a needle by the end with the hole in it. Stroke it thirty times with one prong of the magnet in the same direction every time. Do the same with the second needle, using the same part of the magnet.

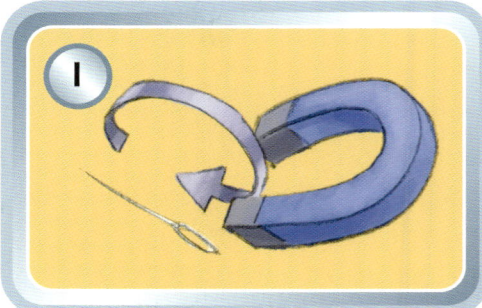

2. Test your needle magnets by picking up drawing pins.

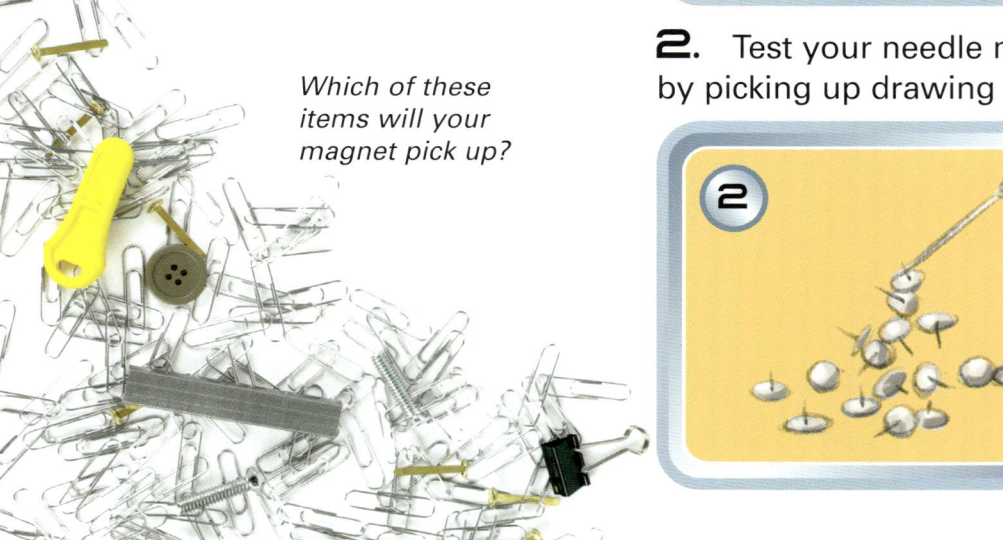

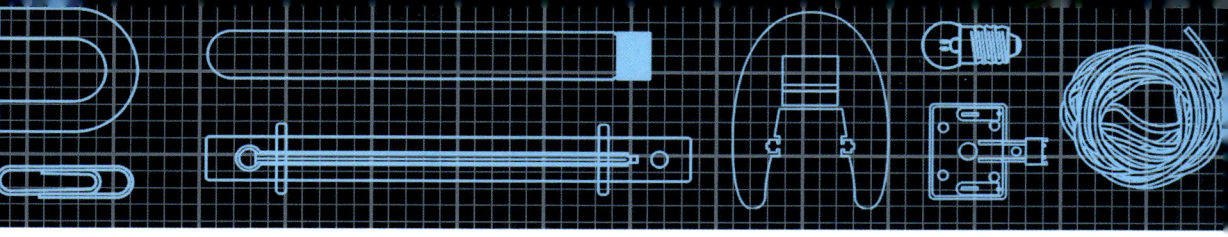

TEST A MAGNET'S STRENGTH

I. Draw a maze on the piece of paper. Put the paperclip on top and the magnet underneath. Use the magnet to guide the paperclip through the maze.

YOU WILL NEED
- a horseshoe magnet
- a piece of paper
- a pen
- a paperclip
- a glass of water
- a plastic or wooden ruler

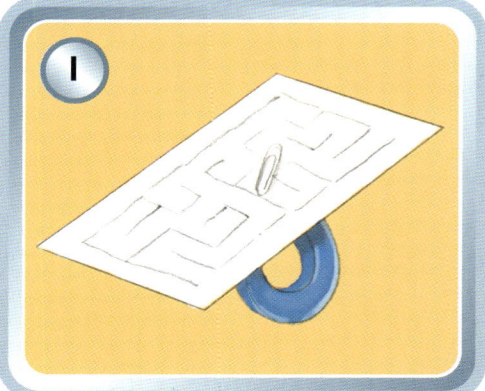

3. See if you can make the paperclip climb up a plastic or wooden ruler using the magnet underneath.

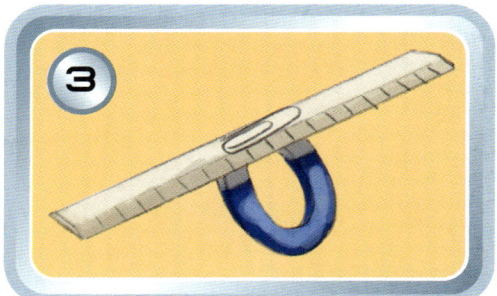

2. Put the paperclip in a glass of water and use the magnet to 'rescue' the paperclip.

PULL AND PUSH

YOU WILL NEED

- two pieces of paper
- the two magnetised needles from page 32
- a bowl of water

I. Carefully balance the magnetised needles on the pieces of paper, then float them in the bowl of water.

2. First, turn them end to end with one pointed end next to the other. What happens? Now try putting the needles eye to eye.

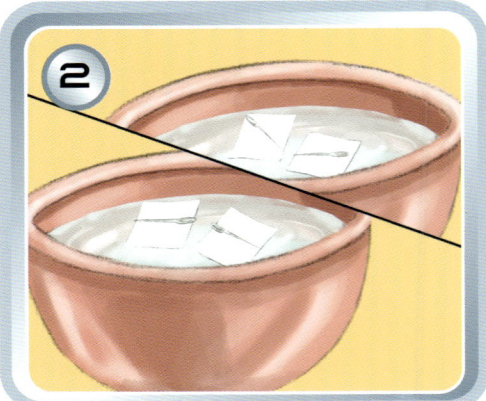

MAGNETIC POLES

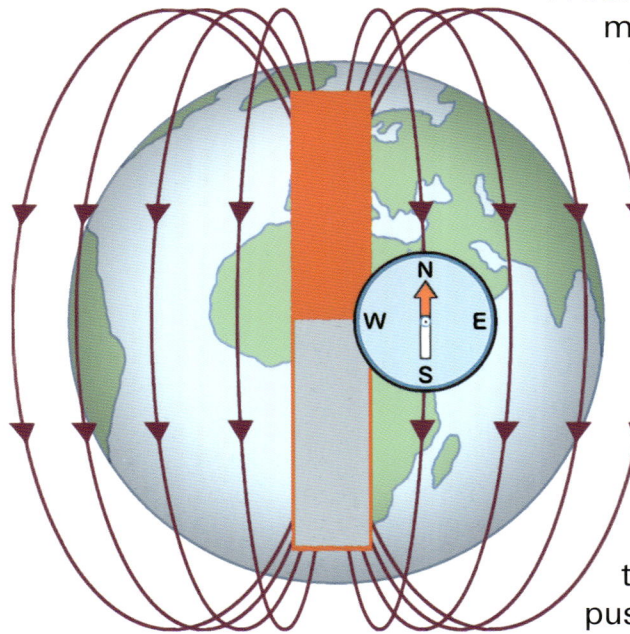

The iron core at the centre of Earth creates a magnetic field. A compass contains a magnetised needle which follows the field, lining up in a north-south direction. Every magnet has two ends, called poles. When you put the poles of two magnets together, they will either pull towards each other (called attraction), or push apart (called repulsion). They pull if they're different, and push if they're the same.

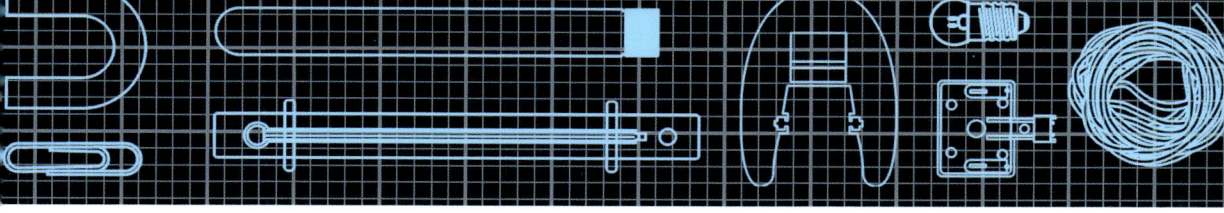

USING ELECTROMAGNETISM

Electromagnetism is all around us and is used in many different ways. Radars use electro-magnetism to send out signals made up of a wave of a particular frequency. A wave-length returned at a certain time is used to find an object.

Loudspeakers use electromagnets to create sound.

Electromagnetism is used to send signals to satellites orbiting Earth.

Giant electromagnets are used in junkyards to shift heavy scrap metal.

Electromagnets can be made much larger than natural magnets which means they can pick up very big objects. When the current is turned off, the magnetism is also turned off.

The loudspeakers in a radio, TV, CD player or computer use a varying electric current passed through an electromagnet in order to create sound.

UNDERSTANDING ELECTROMAGNETISM

Magnetism and electricity are very closely related. When a set of coils is wound around an iron core and electricity is passed through the coils, the iron core becomes a temporary magnet. This is because both electricity and magnetism work in the same way. Electricity has positives and negatives, and magnetism has north and south poles.

MAKE YOUR OWN ELECTROMAGNET

YOU WILL NEED

- 100 cm of insulated copper wire
- scissors
- a large iron or steel nail
- two electrical lead wires with alligator clips at each end
- a battery casing and two AA batteries
- paperclips

1. Use scissors to strip about 2 cm from each end of the insulated wire. Wind the wire around the nail about thirty times.

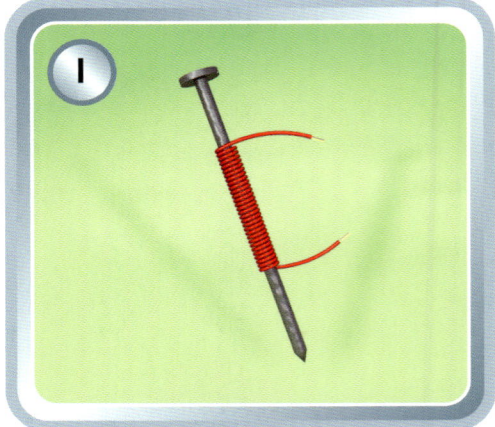

2. Attach a lead wire to each of the bared ends of the insulated wire, then connect them to the battery casing wires.

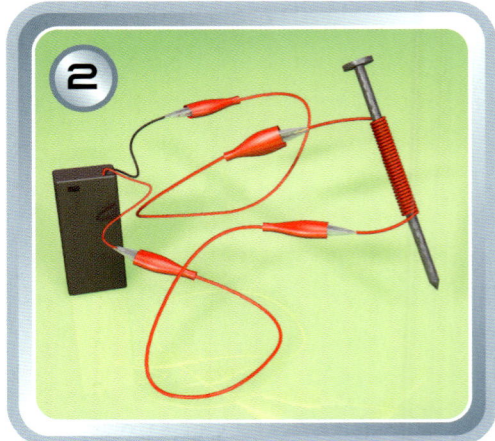

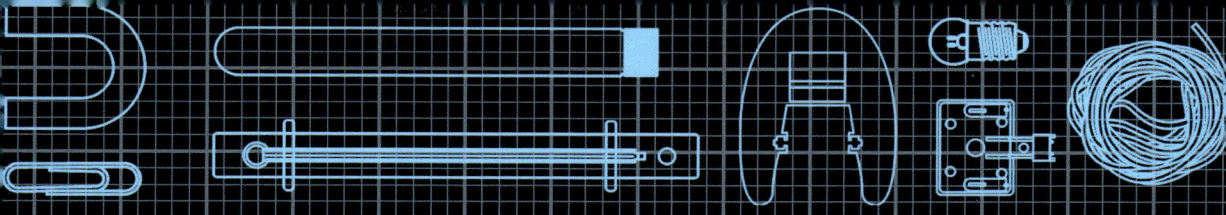

3. Switch on your electromagnet and test it is working by trying to collect the paperclips with the nail.

The more coils of wire there are, the stronger your electromagnet will be. An iron nail will stop being magnetic once the current is switched off, but if the nail is steel, it will remain magnetised.

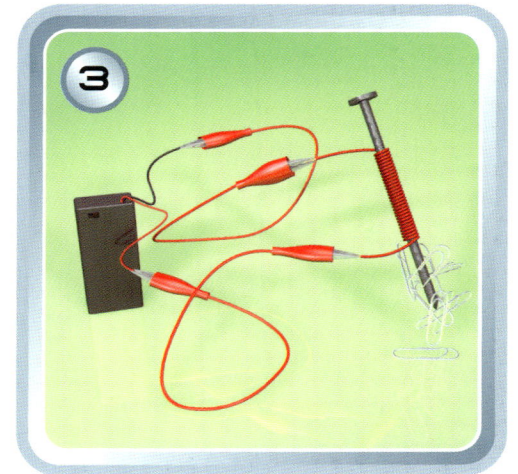

THE BERMUDA TRIANGLE – FACT OR FICTION?

A number of ships and aircraft have mysteriously disappeared in an area near Bermuda known as the Bermuda, or Devil's, Triangle. Nobody really knows what happened to them, but several scientists think that unexplained magnetic fields could have caused erratic compass readings, sending ships and planes off course and into trouble.

United States

Mexico

Bermuda

Miami

BERMUDA TRIANGLE

San Juan

ALTHOUGH BACTERIA CAN SPREAD INFECTION AND BE VERY DANGEROUS, IT'S NOT ALL HARMFUL. WE HAVE BACTERIA IN OUR BODIES THAT HELP US WITH VITAL FUNCTIONS, SUCH AS DIGESTION.

MAKING MOULD

Moulds are microscopic plants that, unlike green plants, make their food by eating other things. Moulds grow on things such as oranges, cheese and bread.

YOU WILL NEED

• soil
• white bread without crusts
• two jars with lids

1. Rub your hands in soil to get them dirty, then wipe them all over some of the bread.

2. Label one jar 'Clean' and put the clean bread inside; label the other jar 'Dirty' and put the soiled bread inside. Tightly close the lids on both jars and put them on a sunny windowsill.

WARNING

Always wash your hands after handling mouldy food, and throw everything away once you have finished with it.

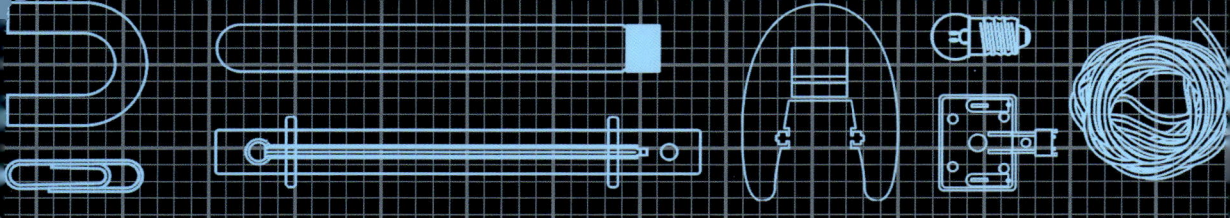

3. Look at the jars after a few days – you should find more mould on the dirty bread than on the clean bread.

HOW DOES IT WORK?

Dirt acts like glue and catches the mould spores. Mould likes warmth, which is why you put the jars by the window in the sun. By sealing the lid, you trapped moisture inside the jar, and mould also likes moisture. Bacteria can also be grown on agar jelly from sneezes, coughs, fingerprints or hairs. Ask an adult to help you do this to see how easily germs are spread.

PENICILLIN

In 1928, Sir Alexander Fleming discovered that the mould *Penicillium notatum* destroyed harmful bacteria. This discovery led scientists to do many experiments until penicillin was safe for humans to use.

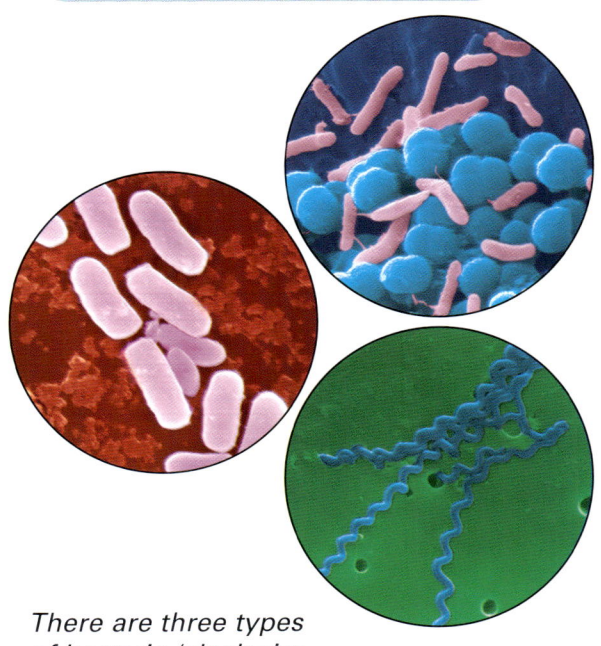

The Penicillium *mould was discovered by Sir Alexander Fleming.*

There are three types of bacteria (clockwise from top right): mixed, spiral and rod.

OUR ATMOSPHERE IS FULL OF WATER VAPOUR. IT CHANGES INTO WATER WHEN IT MEETS A COLD OBJECT – SUCH AS A BOTTLE TAKEN OUT OF THE FRIDGE – AND THIS IS CALLED CONDENSATION. WHEN WATER IS HEATED UP, IT CHANGES BACK INTO A VAPOUR AND THIS IS CALLED EVAPORATION.

TURN SALTY WATER PURE

If water is boiled, it evaporates very fast. Salty water can be turned into pure, drinkable water by being repeatedly evaporated and condensed.

YOU WILL NEED
- a large heat-proof bowl
- boiling water
- salt
- a tablespoon
- food colouring
- clingfilm
- a small heat-proof bowl
- a heavy coin

WARNING
Ask an adult to help you when you're experimenting with boiling water.

I. Pour about 2.5 cm of boiling water into the large bowl. Stir in three tablespoons of salt and some food colouring.

2. Stand the small bowl in the middle of the coloured water. If it floats, carefully tip water out of the large bowl until the small bowl sits on the bottom.

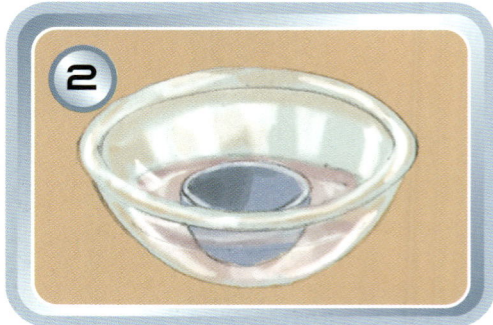

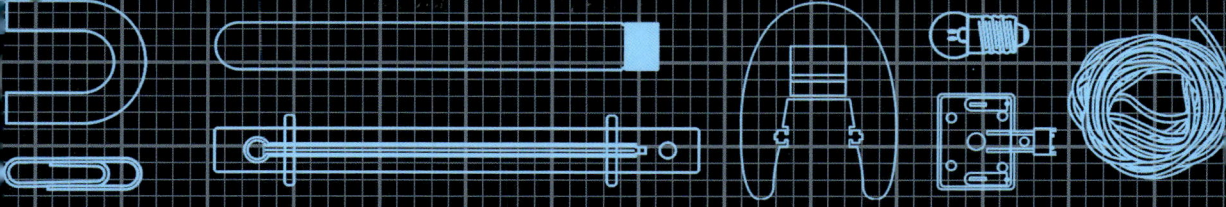

3. Cover the large bowl with the plastic wrap. Put the coin in the middle of the plastic wrap directly above the small bowl. Leave the experiment for about two hours.

4. Peel back the plastic wrap and have a look at your experiment again. Some water should have collected inside the small bowl. What does the water taste like?

Water desalination plants treat salt water to make it safe for drinking. Countries with little rainfall use this type of plant.

HOW DOES IT WORK?

Your experiment works by distillation. The vapour from the boiling salty water evaporates until it meets the clingfilm, where it cools and condenses into pure water. This water drips into the small bowl. So, the water in the little bowl shouldn't be salty.

Did you discover this when you tasted the water?

ARCHIMEDES WAS A MATHEMATICIAN FROM SYRACUSE, ITALY. HE WAS BORN IN 287 BC AND DIED IN 212 BC. AMONGST HIS MANY INVENTIONS AND MATHEMATICAL DISCOVERIES, ARCHIMEDES ESTABLISHED THE ARCHIMEDES PRINCIPLE.

EUREKA!

You may have heard the expression 'Eureka!' used by someone who has made an amazing discovery. It comes from Archimedes. The story goes that Archimedes realised the principle of displacement when his bath overflowed as he climbed into it.

THE ARCHIMEDES PRINCIPLE

'Eureka' means 'I've found it' and it's what Archimedes is thought to have said as he ran naked through the streets following his discovery. Archimedes

Archimedes discovered why things float.

realised that he was heavier than the water in the bath, which was why he had displaced it. Things such as boats – and humans – float and feel lighter in water because of the water pushing against them. The force of the water pushing upwards is called the upthrust. This is equal to the weight of the water that is pushed away by the object.

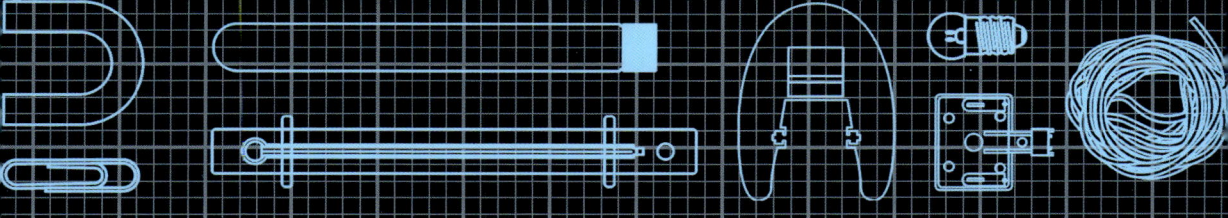

MAKE A SOAP-POWERED BOAT

YOU WILL NEED

- a piece of tinfoil
- scissors
- a bowl of water
- washing-up liquid
- a matchstick or piece of wood.

I. Cut out a piece of foil shaped like a boat and put it on the surface of the water.

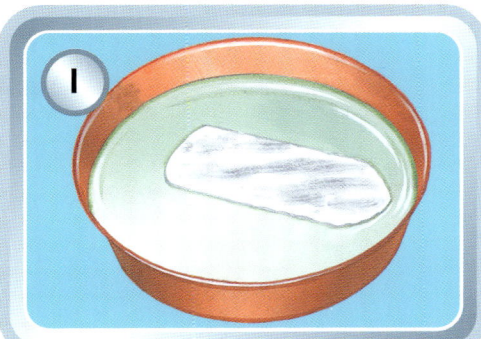

2. Dip the match in washing-up liquid and touch the water just behind the boat.

3. The washing-up liquid breaks the surface tension behind the boat and the reaction carries the boat across the water.

HOW DOES IT WORK?

If you look closely at the surface of any liquid it seems to be covered with an invisible skin. This is caused by surface tension. Soap bubbles are formed when the surface tension of water is weakened.

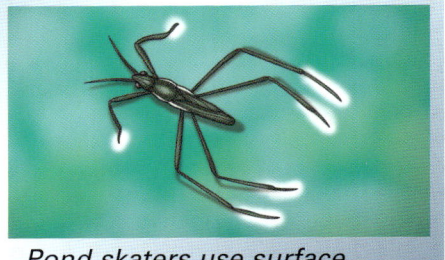

Pond skaters use surface tension to support themselves on the surface of the water.

THE WORD 'PHOTOGRAPHY' COMES FROM THE GREEK WORDS 'PHOTOS' WHICH MEANS 'LIGHT', AND 'GRAPHEIN' WHICH MEANS 'TO DRAW'. IT WAS FIRST USED BY SIR JOHN F W HERSCHEL IN 1839. PHOTOGRAPHY MEANS RECORDING IMAGES USING LIGHT, OR RELATED RADIATION, ON A SENSITIVE MATERIAL.

THE CAMERA OBSCURA

A camera obscura, or pinhole camera, projects an image without using a lens. Most people believe that the camera obscura was first used to observe the Sun and solar eclipses. It began to be used by Renaissance artists, such as Leonardo da Vinci, to help them understand light patterns. The camera obscura works in a dark room or a box with a hole on one side of it. Images from outside the room or box appear upside down on the other side of the hole.

This is an example of an early camera – imagine taking it on holiday!

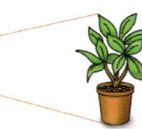

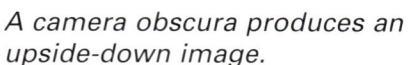

A camera obscura produces an upside-down image.

MAKE A PINHOLE VIEWER

YOU WILL NEED

- a shoebox with a lid
- black paint
- a piece of tracing paper
- scissors
- sticky tape
- a drawing pin

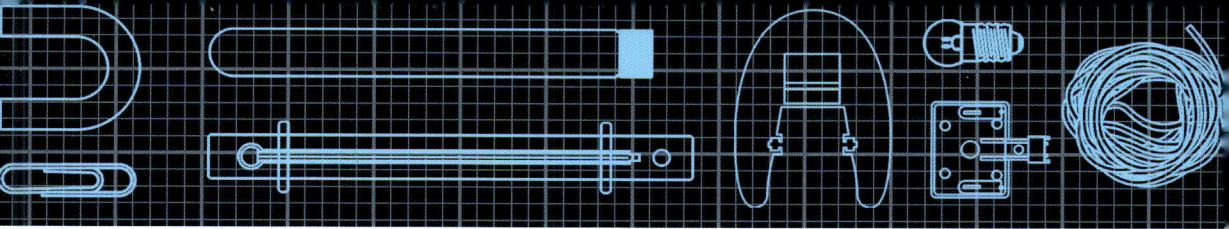

I. Cut out one of the small sides of the shoebox, leaving 2 cm around the edge. Paint the inside of the box black. Tightly tape the lid to the box, making sure no light can get in.

3. Make a tiny hole with the drawing pin in the middle of the end opposite your tracing paper. The smaller the hole, the more sharply focussed the image will appear.

2. Cut a piece of tracing paper about 1.5 cm larger all the way round than the rectangle and tape it over the hole in the side of the box. This is what you'll look at.

4. Stand indoors and point the hole towards the window. Make sure there's no bright light behind you. You should be able to see the image of the window upside down.

ELEMENTS AND COMPOUNDS

THERE ARE ONLY A FEW PURE ELEMENTS IN THE WORLD – GOLD AND SILVER, FOR INSTANCE. WHEN ELEMENTS BOND TOGETHER THEY FORM A COMPOUND. COMPOUNDS AND ELEMENTS CAN MIX TOGETHER WITH NO REACTION TO FORM A SOLUTION.

COMPOUNDS

A compound is very different from the elements that make it, and it is difficult to separate the elements once they have bonded. A good example of a compound is ordinary salt – sodium and chlorine combined to make sodium chloride. On their own, sodium and chlorine are highly poisonous.

Gold is a pure element, while salt (inset) is a compound.

SOLUTIONS

Solutions are mixtures where substances don't separate when they are mixed together. They're usually liquids. A good example is sugar in tea. Here, tea is the solvent and sugar the solute. The maximum amount of any solute that can dissolve in a particular amount of solvent is called its solubility.

Solubility usually depends on the temperature to which the solvent has been heated.

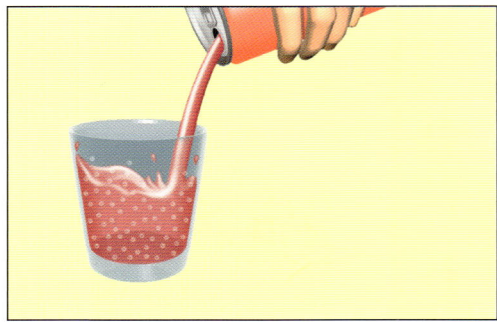

Gases can also be part of a solution – fizzy drinks have carbon dioxide gas and sugar dissolved in water.

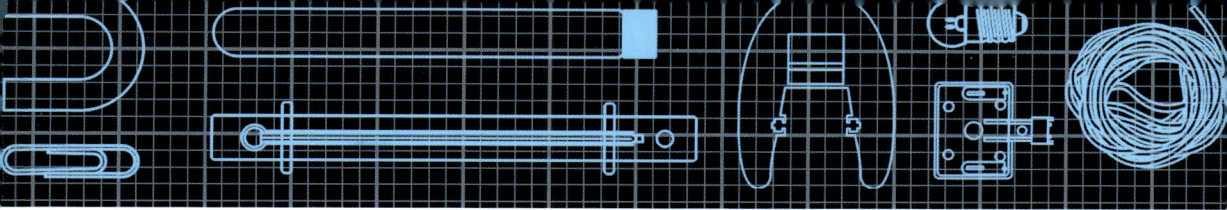

MIXTURES

Solids, liquids and gases can be mixed together to form all kinds of things. Bread, for example, is a mixture of flour (solid), water (liquid) and air (gas). Alcohol and water mix together easily, but other liquids, such as vinegar and oil, separate into two parts.

Bread is formed from solid (flour), liquid (water) and gas (air).

EXPERIMENTING WITH IMMISCIBLE LIQUIDS

Liquids that don't mix together are called immiscible liquids.

YOU WILL NEED
- a test tube or tall glass
- vinegar
- oil (olive or vegetable)
- an egg yolk

I. Pour a small amount of vinegar into the test tube or glass and add a few drops of oil. The two liquids will not mix together. They are immiscible liquids.

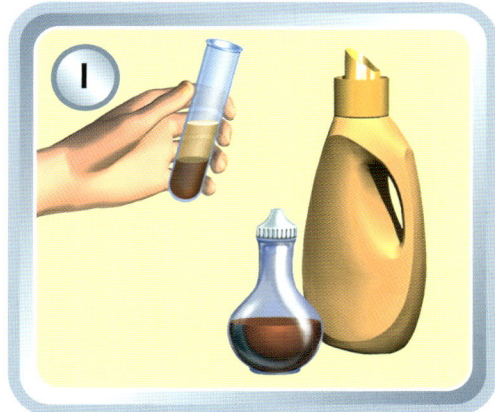

2. Add a small amount of the egg yolk. This will keep the droplets of oil suspended in the vinegar, forming a mixture called emulsion. We know this emulsion as mayonnaise.

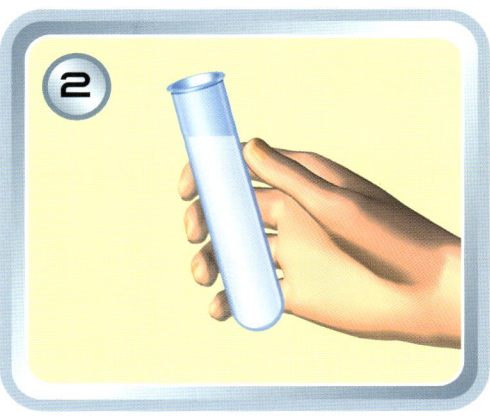

OBSERVING A CHEMICAL REACTION

Chemical reactions occur when one substance is changed to another using chemicals.

YOU WILL NEED

- steel wool
- vinegar
- a test tube, or jar, with a lid

I. Soak the steel wool in vinegar for a minute and then squeeze all the vinegar out. Place the steel wool inside the test tube or jar and close the lid. Leave the wool inside for five minutes.

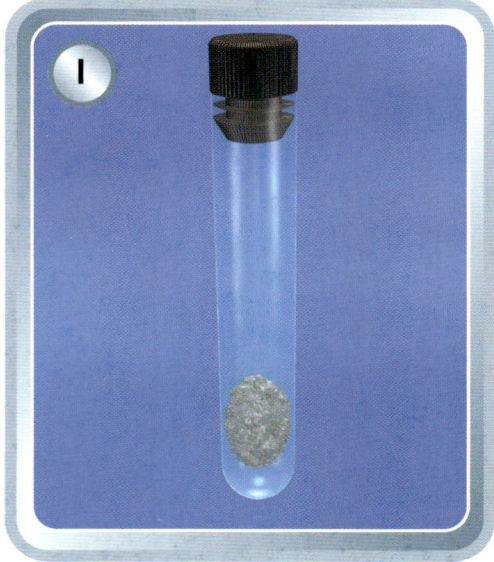

2. Now, feel the test tube – it should have warmed up. This is because the vinegar removes the protective coating from the steel. When this happens, the steel begins to rust and the iron combines with oxygen. This releases heat energy.